Aussie English for Beginners

Book Three

Cartoons by David Pope

NATIONAL
**MUSEUM OF
AUSTRALIA**
C A N B E R R A

First published 2004 by
   National Museum of Australia
   GPO Box 1901
   CANBERRA ACT 2601
   Phone +61 2 6208 5000
   Fax +61 2 6208 5148
   Email information@nma.gov.au
   Website www.nma.gov.au

National Library of Australia cataloguing-in-publication data:
         Pope, David Phillip, 1965- .
         Aussie English for beginners. Book three.

         ISBN 1 876944 25 0

         1. English language - Australia - Caricatures and cartoons.
         2. English language - Australia - Conversation and phrase books.
         I. National Museum of Australia.   II. Australian National
         Dictionary Centre.   III. Title.

         428

Designed and typeset by Roar Creative, Canberra
Printed by Hyde Park Press, Adelaide

Foreword

The National Museum of Australia is all about what it is to be Australian. Why we are what we are, why we are where we are, and how we came to be here. Australian phrases, like the Museum's exhibitions, are a revelation of how our cultural history, national experience and determinedly individualistic approach to life have shaped our identity.

The *Aussie English for Beginners* series is based on one of the most popular exhibits in the National Museum. It explores some of the origins and meanings of many common Australian sayings and, in the true Aussie spirit of a fair go, aims to share their richness with all comers.

Like the first two books in this series, *Aussie English for Beginners Book Three* is a product of collaboration between the National Museum of Australia and the Australian National Dictionary Centre. Each phrase is illustrated by David Pope who, in 2003, won the Australian Cartoonists Association's 'Stanley' award for humorous illustration for his work in previous *Aussie English for Beginners* editions.

So, give it a burl. This book gives you the full bottle on the Australian vernacular. No worries.

Introduction

The first two books in the series *Aussie English for Beginners* focused mainly on single words (such as **bludger, dob, ocker** and **swag**), although there were some idioms (**bring a plate, full as a goog, send her down, Hughie**, and **don't come the raw prawn with me!**). This third book focuses exclusively on idioms.

What is an idiom? An idiom is a group of words that has a meaning that cannot be worked out just from understanding the senses of the individual words. If you look up the word **moon** in a dictionary, it will tell you that the word's primary meaning is 'the natural satellite of the earth, visible (chiefly at night) by light reflected from the sun'. But, if you look up the idiom **over the moon**, you will be told that this means 'extremely happy, delighted'. The relationship between the meanings of the individual words in the idiom and the meaning of the idiom as a whole is not at all self-evident. The origin of this idiom is not entirely certain, but it probably comes from the nursery rhyme line 'the cow jumped over the moon'. Some idioms have quite interesting historical origins. Take the case of the seemingly strange idiom **to steal someone's thunder** meaning 'to take the limelight or attention from another person'. We know that this goes back to the late seventeenth-century English dramatist John Dennis, who invented a new way of creating the effects of thunder on stage only to find that his invention was stolen for use in someone else's play.

Because the meanings of English idioms are not self-evident, they can prove especially difficult for people who are learning English. In Australia, not only do the new English speakers have to learn the idioms of international English, but they also have to learn our own unique Australian idioms. For example, there are some international idioms that describe madness or eccentricity — **mad as a hatter, mad as a march hare** and **mad as a wet hen**. But in Australia, we have many more. What would a non-Australian make of the idioms **silly as a wheel, silly as a chook, silly as a two-bob watch, to have kangaroos in the top paddock, as mad as a gum tree full of galahs, not the full quid** and **short of a sheet of bark?** *Aussie English for Beginners* Book Three tries to make sense of some of the most common Australian idioms.

The process of the creation and loss of idioms is difficult to predict. Although the last trams ran on the Bondi line in Sydney in 1960, the idiom **to shoot through like a Bondi tram** has remained firmly part of Australian English. Some idioms, however, have become dated. For example, the idiom **full up to dolly's wax** means that you have eaten enough — it refers to the time before plastics were widely used, when children's dolls had wax heads attached to cloth bodies. Such dolls have disappeared and the idiom has largely disappeared with it. **I heard it from the man outside Hoyts** is an idiom that was common in Australian English until the 1970s. It originally referred to the commissionaire outside a Hoyts picture theatre in Melbourne in the 1930s. He had the reputation for knowing everything that was going on, so if you heard something from the man outside Hoyts it had to be true! This idiom has almost entirely disappeared from Australian English, as has the Sydney idiom **more hide than Jessie** — a reference to Jessie the elephant (who died in 1939) of Taronga Park Zoo.

Is Australian English continuing to produce new idioms? We toyed with the idea of including the idiom **straight to the poolroom**, a favourite of Darryl Kerrigan (Michael Caton) in the 1997 Australian movie *The Castle*. It is used to refer to something that is regarded as so special that it cannot be used, but must go on display — 'Darl, this Chinese vase you've painted is beautiful — it's going straight to the poolroom'. We are not convinced, however, that the idiom will last. During the Winter Olympics at Salt Lake City in 2002, Steven Bradbury won a gold medal in the short track speed skating competition when all the other skaters fell. In the following months, the phrase **to do a Bradbury** was widely used to describe someone who came from behind to be the unlikely winner of a contest. But the idiom has now almost entirely disappeared. **Not happy, Jan**, from a series of advertisements for the *Yellow Pages* is proving more resilient, and it will be interesting to see if some of the idioms from the ABC television series *Kath and Kim* last beyond the show — for example, **look at moy, look at moy!** and **it's noice, different, unusual**.

A number of the words explored in *Aussie English for Beginners* Books One and Two came from Australian Indigenous languages or from British dialects, both historically important sources for Australian words. In this collection of idioms, there are no Indigenous words and there are very few that have a dialect origin. What we find with idioms is a truly home-grown product. Some of the idioms carry the memory of important Australian historical figures (see **do a Melba** and **such is life**) or events (**your blood's worth bottling** comes from the First World War, whereas **go troppo** comes from the Second World War), but most of them are timeless expressions of quintessential Australian values and attitudes. The typical Australian is prepared to **stir the possum** if necessary, but is more content to live in a world characterised by **no worries** and **she's apples**. The same Australian has a strong sense of injustice — **fair suck of the sauce bottle** — and sympathy for anyone who **gets the rough end of the pineapple**. But there is no sympathy for those who **have tickets on themselves**, are **as flash as a rat with a gold tooth**, or who **wouldn't work in an iron lung**. And there is absolutely no sympathy for those who dare to take you for a fool — see **I didn't come down in the last shower** or **what do you think this is, bush week?**

Most important of all, the words in this book demonstrate a kind of linguistic larrikinism — they show a delight in playing with language and a rebellious rejection of convention. If, after a hard day of physical work in very hot weather, an Aussie walks into the pub and proclaims **I'm as dry as a pommy's towel**, there is here a superb conflation of post-colonial history and laconic Australian humour.

Bruce Moore

Bruce Moore
Director
Australian National Dictionary Centre
Faculty of Arts
Australian National University

be off like a bride's nightie

Depart quickly, move with a sudden burst of
speed. It is likely that this expression was first
used in horseracing to refer to a horse that
moved very quickly out of the starting gates.
The phrase plays on two different meanings of
the verb 'be off': 'be removed' and 'move away'
— 'they took one look at dad's face and were
off like a bride's nightie'.

bottom of the harbour

A tax avoidance scheme. In the late 1970s a
large number of 'bottom of the harbour' schemes
were operating in corporate Australia. The schemes
involved buying a company with a large tax
liability, converting its assets to cash and then
'hiding' the company by, for example, selling it to
a fictitious buyer. Thus the company (and often its
records) vanished completely — figuratively sent
to the 'bottom of the harbour' (originally Sydney
Harbour) — with an unpaid tax bill.

carry on like a pork chop

To make a fuss, to behave in a silly or excited way. This is an elaboration of the standard phrase 'to carry on'. The pork chop is an Australian addition, and some people suggest that the phrase derives from the fact that frying pork makes an especially loud spitting noise. The Australian phrase may have been influenced by the expression 'like a pork chop in a synagogue', meaning 'out of place' or 'unpopular'.

chuck a wobbly

Lose your temper, have a tantrum, as when one federal parliamentarian admonished another in the Senate: 'Stop chucking a wobbly, Senator. Behave yourself'. It is a variation on the earlier phrase 'throw a fit'. 'Chuck', in the sense of 'throw' or 'stage', is used in other Australian expressions with the same meaning, such as 'chuck a mental' and 'chuck a mickey'.

cup of tea, a Bex and a good lie down

A joking term for a cure-all, the remedy for any problem. The phrase (now often with some variations) was originally the title of a 1960s Sydney theatrical revue. The cuppa, the Bex (an analgesic in powder form) and the lie down were supposed to be the suburban housewife's solution to problems such as depression, anxiety, isolation and boredom. The expression is often used in political contexts — 'He called the protesting MPs in for a cup of tea, a Bex and a good lie down'.

do a Melba

Return from retirement to make a number of 'farewell' appearances. The phrase refers to Australian operatic soprano Dame Nellie Melba (Helen Porter Mitchell) 1861–1931, whose stage name derived from her birthplace, Melbourne. She announced her retirement in 1924 but gave 'farewell' performances at Covent Garden in 1926, in Sydney, Melbourne and Geelong in 1928, and then sang in England over the next two years.

done like a dinner

Comprehensively outwitted or defeated —
'Collingwood was done like a dinner in the grand
final'. The phrase was first recorded in 1847.
The origin is uncertain, but a common variation
is 'done like a dog's dinner', which implies a
meal devoured with enthusiasm, and the bowl
licked clean. This may give a clue to the source
of the phrase. If you are done like a dinner,
you are completely and efficiently demolished.

dry as a pommy's towel

Extremely dry. This is a play on various meanings of the word 'dry'. The phrase can refer to rainless weather or to an arid landscape, but it is most commonly used to mean 'thirsty', especially in expressing a desire for a drink of beer. The phrase derives from the stereotypical Australian view of the English as reluctant to wash, and belongs with other anti-English terms such as 'whingeing pom' and 'full as a pommy's complaint box'.

ducks on the pond

Look out — female approaching! A warning cry from a male as a signal to other men that a woman is approaching a traditionally all-male environment. It is a reminder that the men should modify their language and behaviour to avoid giving offence. It was first used in shearing sheds but is now heard in other places, especially in a pub.

fair suck of the sauce bottle

Steady on, be reasonable. This is one of several
variations on the Australian exclamation 'fair go'.
It expresses a keen sense of injustice — 'fair suck
of the sauce bottle, mate, I'm only asking for a
loan till payday!' Sometimes 'saveloy' or 'sav'
is substituted for 'sauce bottle'. The phrase
'fair crack of the whip' has the same meaning.

fit as a mallee bull

Extremely strong and healthy. A mallee bull is one that lives in mallee country — poor, dry country where small scrubby eucalypts called 'mallee' grow. Any creature that survives in such difficult conditions would have to be tough and fit. 'Forty pushups every morning Kev — you'll be fit as a mallee bull.' The word 'mallee' probably comes from an Aboriginal language of western Victoria.

flash as a rat with a gold tooth

Ostentatious, showy and a bit too flashily dressed. This phrase is used only of a man and implies that, although he may be well-dressed and well-groomed, there is also something a bit dodgy about him. In spite of a superficial smartness, he is not to be trusted. In spite of the gold tooth, he is still a rat.

flat out like a lizard drinking

Extremely busy, at top speed. This is word play on two different meanings of the standard English 'flat out'. The literal sense is to lie fully stretched out (like a lizard), and the figurative sense means as fast as possible. The phrase also alludes to the rapid tongue-movement of a drinking lizard. It is sometimes shortened, as in 'we're flat out like a lizard trying to meet the deadline'.

the full bottle

Knowledgeable, an expert — 'Does Robbo know anything about paving?' 'Yeah mate, he's the full bottle.' The probable source of the phrase is the nineteenth-century British term 'no bottle' ('no good'), an abbreviation of rhyming slang 'no bottle and glass' ('no class'). In Australia 'the full bottle' came to mean 'very good', and then 'very good at, knowledgeable about (something)'. It is often used in the negative — 'not the full bottle' means 'not good (at something)' or 'not fully informed'.

get a guernsey

Gain recognition, be rewarded. In standard
English a guernsey is a thick jumper made from
oiled navy-blue wool, originally from the Isle of
Guernsey. In Australia it came to be applied to
the jumpers worn by Australian Rules football
players — and if you 'got a guernsey' this meant
you had won a place in the team. Later, the phrase
was used to recognise success in any field —
'Nicole Kidman should get a guernsey in this
year's Oscars'.

get the rough end of the pineapple

Get a raw deal, be treated badly — 'Sally got the sack? She really got the rough end of the pineapple!' The force of the phrase derives partly from the fact that either end of a pineapple is 'rough', although the end with the prickly leaves is very rough indeed. The equivalent American saying is 'to get the fuzzy end of the lollypop'. The expression was first recorded in the 1960s.

give it a burl

Give it a try, make an attempt. 'Burl' is one of almost 200 words that Australian English borrowed from British dialects. It is a Scots word for a 'spin' or 'whirl', and in Australia we have varied the standard English 'give it a whirl' by replacing the last word with the Scots 'burl': 'The mower should start now Mum — give it a burl!'

go troppo

Behave strangely, lose your mind. The phrase, first used by Australian troops in the Pacific during the Second World War, arose from the idea that long exposure to tropical conditions affected your sanity. It is now used in various contexts — 'Why's Ray selling his house and buying shares in a wind farm?' 'Dunno. Probably gone troppo.' The abbreviation of 'tropical' and the addition of -o demonstrate a common Australian way of altering words.

have tickets on yourself

Be conceited, have a high opinion of yourself —
'He's got tickets on himself if he thinks I'll go
out with him'. The original meaning of 'ticket'
is uncertain, but it may refer to betting tickets
(a person is so conceited that he backs himself),
to raffle tickets, to a high price tag (especially
one on the outfit of a mannequin in a shop
window), or to prize ribbons awarded at an
agricultural show.

I didn't come down in the last shower

I'm not stupid, don't try and put one over me! This is a response to someone who is taking you for a fool. The phrase indicates that you have more experience or shrewdness than you have been given credit for — 'A thousand bucks to paint the laundry? I didn't come down in the last shower!' It was first recorded in the early 1900s.

life wasn't meant to be easy

A catchphrase popularised by Malcolm Fraser (Prime Minister 1975–83) and later attributed by him to the British playwright George Bernard Shaw. The phrase is now used as a stock response to complaints or whinges of any kind — 'I have to take the kids to soccer training every night this week.' 'Well, life wasn't meant to be easy!' Shaw's full quotation is 'life is not meant to be easy, my child; but take courage: it can be delightful'.

like a drover's dog

'Drover's dog' has been used since the 1940s in various similes, usually uncomplimentary — 'a head like a drover's dog' (big and ugly), 'all prick and ribs like a drover's dog' (lean and hungry), and 'leaking like a drover's dog' (as in 'the NSW Cabinet is leaking like a drover's dog!'). It can also mean a nonentity, as when a politician commented in 1983 that 'a drover's dog could lead the Labor Party to victory'.

like a shag on a rock

Isolated, lonely, exposed. A shag is a cormorant, commonly found in coastal and inland waters of Australia, where they are often seen perched alone on a rock. Any isolated person can be described as, or feel like, a shag on a rock — for example, a political leader with few supporters, or a person without friends at a party.

like a stunned mullet

Dazed, confused, bewildered. The phrase, first recorded in the 1950s, alludes to the goggle-eyed stare (and sometimes gaping mouth) of a fish that has been recently caught and made unconscious. A person typically looks like a stunned mullet as the result of a sudden shock or surprise.

mad as a cut snake

Crazy or angry. The two senses of the phrase derive from the fact that 'mad' has two main senses — 'crazy' and 'angry'. The 'crazy' sense is illustrated by 'that bloke wearing a teapot on his head is as mad as a cut snake', and the angry sense is illustrated by 'be careful of the boss this afternoon, he's as mad as a cut snake'.

may your chooks turn into emus and kick your dunny down

A comic curse. This expression recalls an earlier time when many Australians kept chooks in the back yard and the dunny was a separate outhouse. A similar comic exaggeration is seen in the phrase 'he couldn't train a choko vine over a country dunny' — a comment on a person's incompetence.

miserable as a bandicoot

Extremely unhappy. Bandicoots are small marsupials with long faces, and have been given a role in Australian English in similes that suggest unhappiness or some kind of deprivation. The expression 'miserable as a bandicoot' was first recorded in 1845. A person can also be as 'bald as a bandicoot', as 'blind as a bandicoot', or be isolated 'like a bandicoot on a burnt ridge'.

not know whether you are Arthur or Martha

To be in a state of confusion, as in this comment in an Australian state parliament — 'The Leader of the Opposition does not know whether he is Arthur or Martha, Hekyll or Jekyll, coming or going'. The phrase was first recorded in 1957. In recent years it has also been used with reference to gender confusion, and in this sense it has been exported to other countries.

not within a bull's roar

Not anywhere near — 'The club's not within a
bull's roar of winning the premiership this
season'. A roaring bull can be heard over a great
distance, so that to be 'not within a bull's roar' is
to be a considerable distance away. The phrase
is sometimes used without the negative — to be
'within a bull's roar' means that you are not too
far away. A much finer unit of measurement is
expressed by the similar Australian phrase within
'a bee's dick'.

not a brass razoo

No money at all. A razoo is a non-existent coin of trivial value. The origin of the term is unknown, although it is possibly a corruption of the French coin called a sou. The expression is always used in the negative — 'We did all the fundraising ourselves. Not a brass razoo came from the government'. The brass of 'brass razoo' was no doubt influenced by the British brass farthing. The phrase often appears in the form 'not worth a brass razoo' meaning 'worth nothing at all'.

no worries

That's fine, okay, no problem. This colloquial version of the phrase 'not to worry' is very common in Australia, and also occurs in other forms such as 'no worries, mate', 'no wuckers', and 'nurries'. It implies that everything will come right, or be taken care of, and that we should all be relaxed — 'Will you help me do my homework, Dad? It's due tomorrow!' 'No worries, darl.'

on the sheep's back

A reference to the wool industry as the source of Australia's prosperity, first recorded in 1894. For much of its history, Australia depended on wool as its main export and so the notion arose that Australia was 'riding on the sheep's back'. Although wool is now less important as an export, the phrase still evokes a sense of the importance of the agricultural industry to the country's wealth.

on the turps

Drinking heavily. 'Turps' is an abbreviation of 'turpentine' and the phrase alludes to the use of spirits such as turps and methylated spirits ('metho') by down-and-out alcoholics. In the earliest uses of the phrase, the alcohol referred to is a spirit such as gin or rum, but more recently it has referred to any kind of alcoholic drink, especially beer.

on the wallaby track

On the move, travelling around. The expression
was first recorded in 1849. It is often abbreviated
to 'on the wallaby' — 'Marg and Jim have
bought a new camper and gone on the wallaby'.
The phrase originally referred to the days when
people needed to travel around the country
looking for seasonal work, as though following
a track worn by wallabies heading for a
waterhole or food.

put the hard word on

Ask forcefully for something in the expectation that you will not be refused. Originally the phrase was used of a man propositioning a woman, and was first recorded in 1923. It is now also applied to any manner of heavy-handed requests — 'Michelle really put the hard word on me for a loan of the car'.

rattle your dags

Hurry up, get a move on. Dags are clumps of matted wool and dung which hang around a sheep's rear end. When a 'daggy' sheep runs, the dried dags knock together to make a rattling sound. The word 'dag' (originally 'daglock') was a British dialect word that came into mainstream Australian English in the late nineteenth century.

she's apples

Everything is fine, all is well. Australian English often uses the feminine pronoun 'she' where standard English would use 'it'. For example, instead of 'it'll be right' Australians say 'she'll be right'. 'She's apples' was originally rhyming slang — 'apple and spice' or 'apple and rice' for 'nice'. The phrase has now lost all connection with its rhyming slang origin.

shoot through like a Bondi tram

Make a hasty departure. Bondi is the Sydney suburb renowned worldwide for its surf beach. The phrase (first recorded in 1945) probably derives from the fact that two trams typically left the city for Bondi together, the first an express tram which would 'shoot through' from Darlinghurst to Bondi Junction. Trams last ran on the line in 1960, but the phrase has remained a part of Australian English.

stacks on the mill

In sporting contexts, a pile-up of players, usually on top of the ball. It was originally a schoolyard game, a call to children to pile in a heap on top of someone. The full cry in the Australian children's game was 'stacks on the mill, more on still!' The phrase is now sometimes abbreviated to 'stacks on'. 'Stacks' is a corruption of 'sacks', from an older British game 'more sacks to the mill'.

stir the possum

Deliberately cause controversy, especially in a public debate. The phrase was first recorded in 1900, but its origin is unknown. Some suggest it arose from a reversal of the American expression 'to play possum', which refers to the popular belief that the American possum feigns death when attacked. To 'stir' in Australian English is to deliberately cause trouble or tease someone.

a stubby short of a sixpack

Not very bright or clever, not quite 'with it'.
This is an Australian variation of a common
international idiom, typically represented by
'a sandwich short of a picnic'. It combines the
Australian 'stubby' (a small squat 375 ml bottle
of beer) with the borrowed American 'sixpack'
(a pack of six cans of beer), demonstrating
how readily Australian English naturalises
Americanisms.

such is life

The last words spoken by the bushranger Ned Kelly before he was hanged at Melbourne Gaol in 1880. The phrase is used to express a philosophical acceptance of the bad things that happen in life. It was further popularised by its use as the title for Joseph Furphy's famous novel about rural Australia (1903). Some claim that Kelly's last words were in fact 'Ah well, I suppose it has come to this' — not quite as memorable.

things are crook in Tallarook

This is a catchphrase for any bad situation, formed from a rhyme on the placename. Its use often prompts a similar response from a listener, such as 'but things are dead at Birkenhead'. Other similar Australian rhyming phrases include 'there's nothin' doin' at Araluen', 'got the arse at Bulli Pass', 'in jail at Innisfail', 'things are weak at Julia Creek', and 'there's no lucre at Echuca'.

VERANDAH OVER
THE TOY SHOP

FLAT SCREEN OVER
THE PLAY STATION

verandah over the toy shop

A man's beer belly. 'Toy shop' is a joking term for the male genitals. In standard English 'verandah' is 'an open-sided roofed structure along the outside of a house'. In Australia it also has the sense 'a roof over the pavement in front of a shop, supported by poles', but this sense is in decline since Australian shops now rarely have such verandahs. The more common version of this phrase is now 'awning over the toy shop'.

we'll all be rooned

We will all be ruined. 'Rooned' is a comic representation of broad Irish-Australian speech. The saying is from the refrain of the poem 'Said Hanrahan', published in 1921 by John O'Brien, the pen name of PJ Hartigan. Hanrahan is a farmer who predicts disaster whatever the conditions — 'We'll all be rooned,' said Hanrahan, 'before the year is out'. The expression is now used to mock the pessimists.

what do you think this is, bush week?

Do you think I'm stupid? An indignant response to someone who is taking you for a fool — 'You're going to charge me *how much*? What do you think this is, bush week?' 'Bush week' is a time when country people come to town, and the phrase implies that they are easily fooled by the more sophisticated city slickers. The speaker resents being mistaken for a country bumpkin.

a wigwam for
a goose's bridle

A snubbing reply to an unwanted question. It might be used to answer an inquisitive child who asks 'What's in the bag?' The original English idiom was 'a whim-wham for a goose's bridle'. 'Whim-wham' meaning 'an ornament' disappeared from the language in the nineteenth century and survived only in this phrase. In Australia the meaningless 'whim-wham' was altered to the more familiar 'wigwam', and sometimes to 'wing-wong'.

wouldn't work in an iron lung

Extraordinarily lazy. The phrase derives from the artificial respirator that kept polio patients alive by 'breathing' for them in the days when up to 10,000 people annually were affected by poliomyelitis ('infantile paralysis') in Australia. When vaccinations became routine in the mid-1950s, the fear of polio disappeared. Barry Humphries commented in 1974: 'Work! Brits couldn't even spell it. Bloody poms couldn't work in an iron lung'.

you right?

Do you need my help? Many a foreign visitor, entering an Australian shop, is bemused by the greeting of the sales assistant — 'you right?' Although informal, this is not a sign of disrespect. It is the Australian equivalent of the standard query 'are you being served?' or 'can I help you?' It is short for 'are you all right?'

your blood's worth bottling

You're a really valuable person! You're a loyal friend! This is one of the many Australianisms, along with terms such as 'digger', 'Anzac' and 'Aussie', that arose during the First World War. It applied to a person of great heart, who displayed courage, loyalty, and mateship. It is now used in many contexts: 'Those firefighters — their blood's worth bottling!'

The Australian National Dictionary Centre

The text accompanying the cartoons was provided by members of the Australian National Dictionary Centre in the Faculty of Arts at the Australian National University. The Australian National Dictionary Centre was established in 1988. It conducts research into all aspects of Australian English and provides Oxford University Press with editorial expertise for their range of Australian dictionaries. The Centre was built on ten years of pioneering work which resulted in the publication in 1988 of *The Australian National Dictionary: A Dictionary of Australianisms based on Historical Principles*, the only comprehensive and documented dictionary of Australianisms. The Centre is located in the Faculty of Arts at the Australian National University. It is jointly funded by Oxford University Press and the Australian National University.

The database of the Australian National Dictionary Centre contains a unique collection of Australianisms supported by historical citations. It is this database that lends authority to the Centre's work on Australian English. The Centre has produced a number of  specialist studies of aspects of Australian English. It has published books on regional Australian English (Western Australia, Tasmania, and Queensland), on Aboriginal English, and on thematic topics such as the convict and goldrush eras. For more information on the Centre, see the webpage at www.anu.edu.au

About the cartoonist

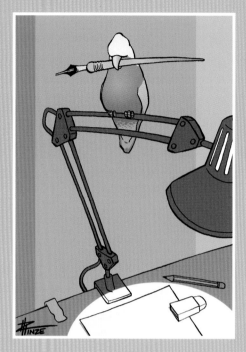

David Pope is a Canberra-based freelance cartoonist best known for the political cartoons he draws for the alternative press in Australia.

He is the author of three books of cartoons: *The fish John West reject* (1995), *Australia Incorporated* (1997) and *Hinzebrand: political cartoons in brine* (2000).

His award-winning work has also appeared in the National Museum of Australia's periodic exhibitions of political humour.

You can visit David on the world wide web at www.scratch.com.au

The National Museum of Australia

The National Museum of Australia tells the stories of people, events and issues that have shaped and influenced our nation. As well as using artefacts as the focus of its stories and exhibitions, the Museum utilises cutting-edge communication technologies. The core exhibitions found within the Museum are:

- Tangled Destinies: Land and People in Australia

- Nation: Symbols of Australia

- Eternity: Stories from the Emotional Heart of Australia

- Horizons: The Peopling of Australia since 1788

- First Australians: Gallery of Aboriginal and Torres Strait Islander Peoples.

Aussie English
for Beginners

Cartoons by David Pope

National Museum of Australia

Aussie English
for Beginners

Book Two

Cartoons by David Pope

National Museum of Australia